FAMILY HISTORY PATCHES

The Stonors

P J Jefferies

Bulmershe College of Higher Education, Reading

D1795956

General editors: D J Steel & L Taylor

Nelson

Thomas the Heir

Introduction

This book tells the story of a family called Stonor, who lived more than 500 years ago. The house, where they lived, Stonor Park near Henley in Oxfordshire, is still there and you can go and see it. What is more there are Stonors, the descendants of the people in this book, who own the house today.

Nowadays we call the century in which our story takes place, the fifteenth century, and the time the Middle Ages. These are only names. To the people then, the time they lived in was 'now', just as our time is 'now' to us. Read the book and try to imagine you are one of the people in it, so that you can feel what it was like to be alive in the Middle Ages.

The family tree of the main people in this book

Thomas Stonor I = Alice Kirby
   Born 1394
   Died 1431

Thomas Stonor II = Jane de la Pole
   Born 1424
   Died 1474

William Stonor = Elizabeth Ryche
   Born 1449
   Died 1494

Orphan Thomas

In 1404 Thomas Stonor, an ancestor of the present-day Stonors, was an orphan boy of 10. An orphan is someone without a father or a mother, or without both. His father, Ralph, had died when Thomas was a baby. Ralph was a young soldier, who went to Ireland with the army of King Richard II and died a few weeks after he got there. Then Thomas's elder brother Gilbert died in 1396, and so Thomas became the heir of the family.

A new family

A few years after Ralph died, Thomas's mother married again and had some more children. So Thomas had a family again.

The pictures show fifteenth-century children playing together. What toys have they got? In what ways are they like modern ones? In what ways are they different?

Look at the family tree on this page. In what year did Ralph go to Ireland? How old were Ralph and Gilbert when they died? What relation are John, Edmund and Isabel to Thomas?

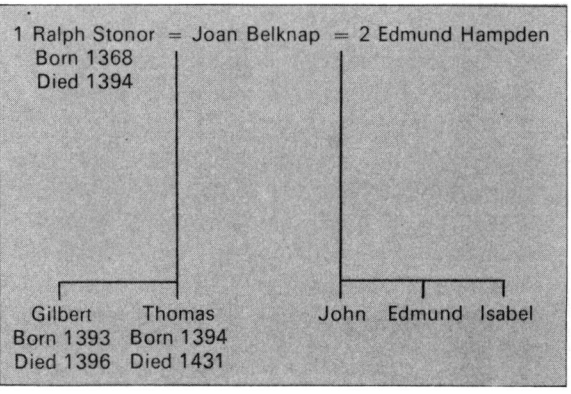

1 Ralph Stonor = Joan Belknap = 2 Edmund Hampden
Born 1368
Died 1394

Gilbert	Thomas		John	Edmund	Isabel
Born 1393	Born 1394				
Died 1396	Died 1431				

The Stonor arms

Thomas Stonor's family were gentry. They were not as rich as barons and lords, but much better off than ordinary working people. Thomas was proud of his ancestors — the members of his family who had lived before him. Some had fought for the king and had been made knights like his father. Some had been made knights because they served the king in other ways.

One of these was a famous judge, Sir John Stonor. Thomas went to see Sir John's tomb in the Abbey Church at Dorchester-on-Thames. The tomb is still there and although there is no name on it, you can tell it belongs to one of the Stonor family by a special mark.

Imagine you are telling a friend how to recognise the tomb when he goes to Dorchester. What is the special mark? Yes, the Stonor arms.

These arms are rather like badges. Originally they were painted on shields in battle so that a man could be easily recognised. But by the time of young Thomas Stonor they were called coats of arms, and families were very proud of them. They showed them off wherever they could — in glass windows, on the silver (plate and cutlery), embroidered on cushions and carved on walls of houses.

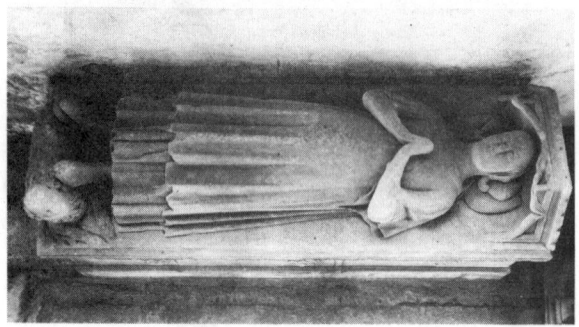

There is an inn in the village of Stonor called The Stonor Arms. Are there any inns or hotels near you with names like that? Find more coats of arms in your own neighbourhood by looking in churches, old houses and museums. Not only families have coats of arms. You can find them in town halls, on china, embroidered on blazers. What is your school badge? Has it got writing on it, or only a picture? What does it mean? See how many coats of arms you can find with animals in them. What is the Queen's coat of arms? When you have finished, see if you can beat the list on page 47.

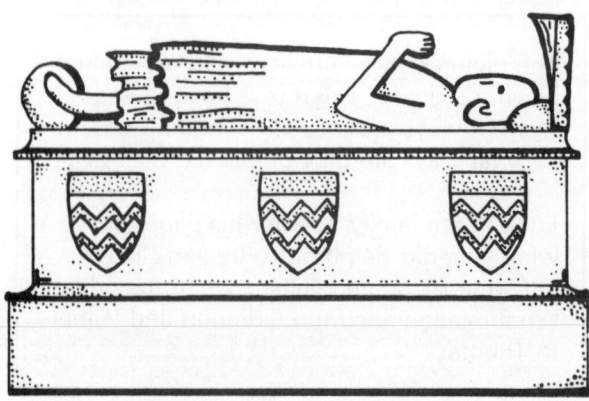

The brass of Thomas Chaucer and his wife in Ewelme church

Thomas's guardian

As well as his family, Thomas had a guardian, Thomas Chaucer, who was his close friend all his life. The reason for this was that Gilbert Stonor had died, so he was the heir and he was rich. When he was 21, he would have his father's house, all his lands and everything he had owned. Meanwhile, he was too young to manage his own affairs, so his guardian looked after all these things (his inheritance); he also advised on Thomas's education and even whom he should marry. Thomas Chaucer did not live in the same house as young Thomas Stonor, but nearby at Ewelme. He was an important man in the government and son of the great English writer, Geoffrey Chaucer.

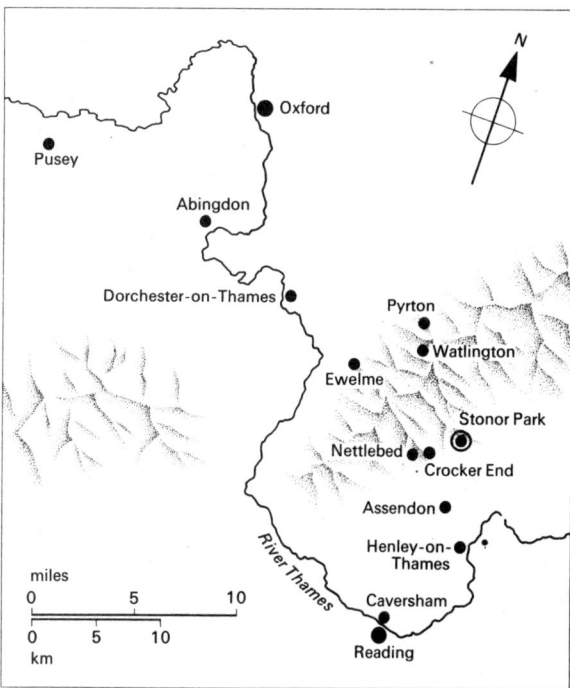

Make up a coat of arms for yourself and your family. Think carefully what things show best what your family is like. You could make a pun. Many coats of arms include puns. For instance, the one for the City of Oxford shows an *ox* passing over a *ford* of water.

You can find Stonor Park and Ewelme on the map on this page. How far is Ewelme from Stonor Park? Remember that Thomas and his guardian would take the short cut across the hills on horseback. How often do you think they would have visited each other?

Thomas's education

Thomas learnt to read and write English, Latin and French. Latin and French were still the languages used for many documents, letters and books. Thomas could read his grandfather's letters written in Latin and French, which were kept in a large oak chest.

This is how one of the letters to Thomas's grandfather began:

'Trecher sire et amy . . .'

In modern English it would be: 'Very dear sir and friend . . .'

Find out how the beginning of the letter would be written in modern French.

French had been the fashionable language for people to speak in England for over 300 years. Why do you think this was? However, by the time Thomas Stonor was born, more and more people were talking and writing in English. One of the people who helped this change was Geoffrey Chaucer, who wrote *The Canterbury Tales* in English. He was the first great English writer. As Thomas Stonor's guardian was Chaucer's son, you may be sure that Thomas read *The Canterbury Tales* and very good stories they are too.

Schoolboys did have spelling lessons in Thomas Stonor's time but they had very few books and did not use a dictionary, so their spelling was erratic. (Is yours?) The books Thomas Stonor used were copied by hand and a few had pictures and illuminations like some of the pictures in this book.

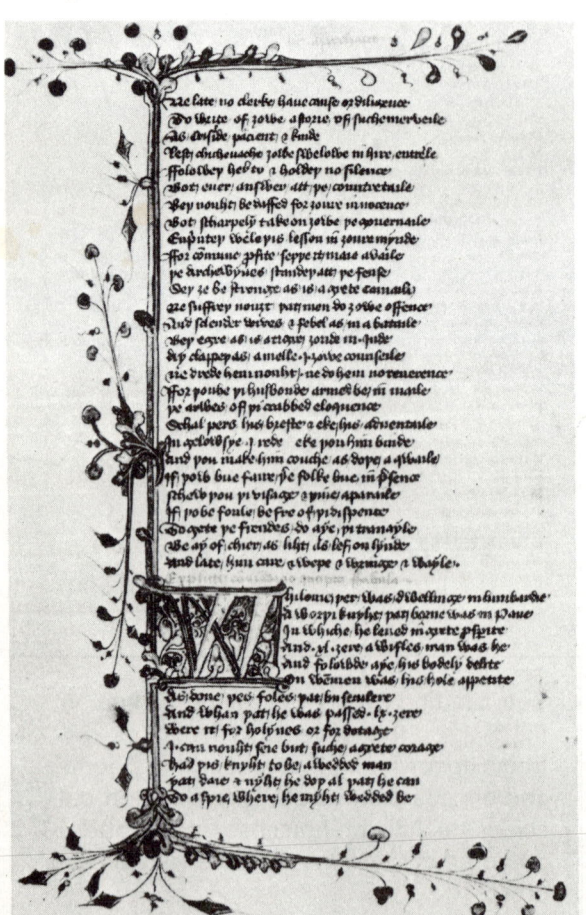

Geoffrey Chaucer
(left) A page from The Canterbury Tales

Pounds, shillings and pence

Thomas also needed to learn arithmetic so that he would be able to check the accounts. Here is one of the accounts he paid when he grew up.

Paid to the smith		*xid*
Paid for two fishes		*iid*
Paid to Ralph the Fool		*iid*
Paid for half a beef	*vs*	*iiiid*
Paid for bread	*viiis*	
Paid for wine		*xxiid*
Paid for a brawn	*iiis*	*iiiid*
	————	————
Total	*xix*	*ix*

(s = shillings d = pence)

You will notice that the money is written in Roman numerals. Learning these was easy. But his £ was not divided up in the same way as ours. Thomas would have understood how the moneyer (the man licensed by the king to make coins) made silver pennies. He weighed out a pound (554 grammes) of silver, and he had to hammer it out flat to just the right size for cutting out 240 little silver pennies, rather like making jam tarts. He had to be good at it, so that he would get each coin equal in weight with no waste and he had to be honest too! So Thomas Stonor's money was like this:

> 12 pennies (pence) = 1 shilling
> 20 shillings = 1 pound
>
> So 240 pence = 1 pound

Sometimes Thomas did sums with counters, and sometimes he used the same numerals as we do. Both are in the picture.

Ask your parents when the shillings and old pence stopped being used. What is the difference between an old penny and a new penny? Try and work out what the total for Thomas Stonor's account would be in new pence.

Write your age in Roman numerals. Then write the day of the month, the year, and how much pocket money you get, all in Roman numerals.

So much to learn

Thomas was taught some things which we are not taught today. He had to learn how to manage his estates. What were the best crops to grow on his fields? What were the best kind of sheep and horses? What sort of men should he employ? How many houses and farm tenants did he have?

Then he had to know something about the law. He could employ a lawyer, of course, but he had to know what to do if someone tried to steal some of his land. He was not a judge, but it was part of his duty as landlord to keep the peace. He would be expected to deal with small crimes on his own estates, and, if asked to by the King, with more serious ones in Oxfordshire.

He learnt to ride a horse, to shoot with a bow and arrow, to use a sword, and how to wear armour without being too uncomfortable. He also learnt which wines to choose, and good table manners. Have you ever made a list of all the things you will have to learn? If you do, you may be surprised; you may find the list is just as long as it was for Thomas Stonor — or even longer. And do you learn all these things at school?

Thomas learnt many things at home, and one of the most important was religion.

The priests

Religious education was taken for granted in Thomas Stonor's England. He was a Roman Catholic because at that time all Christians in western Europe were members of one church, with its headquarters in Rome and its leader the Pope. The Stonors had a private chapel right by the house, with a special set of rooms for the priests to live in. People who could afford it, often built themselves these private chapels, partly for their own comfort and partly because they thought God wanted them to do it. So Thomas really had a small private monastery with six priests whom he housed and fed.

The priests could teach Thomas Bible stories, the lives of the saints, prayers and help him to understand the church services, which were in Latin. They could teach him French and arithmetic as well.

Schools

Some boys went away to school, perhaps to be taught by the monks at the great abbeys of Reading or Abingdon. Thomas Stonor's uncle had been to a boarding school in Oxford, and already new schools were being founded called Grammar Schools, such as the one at Sevenoaks in Kent.

> How old is your school?
> Are there any very old schools near you?
> Some started a long time ago but are now in new buildings. Ask your teacher to help you find out about this.

Master of Stonor park

Thomas Stonor continued to listen to his guardian, Thomas Chaucer's advice all his life. However, once he came of age, that is, when he was twenty-one years old, he could make decisions for himself.

> How old do you have to be now to come of age? What does it mean?

In 1415 he did two important things. He got married and decided to make his house at Stonor bigger. If you go to it now, you will see one large house (look at the picture on page 2).

Inside it is Thomas Stonor's house. In order to understand what it was like, you have to imagine youself taking away some of the walls, like peeling layers off an onion. Then you would see the buildings as they were when Thomas Stonor lived there.

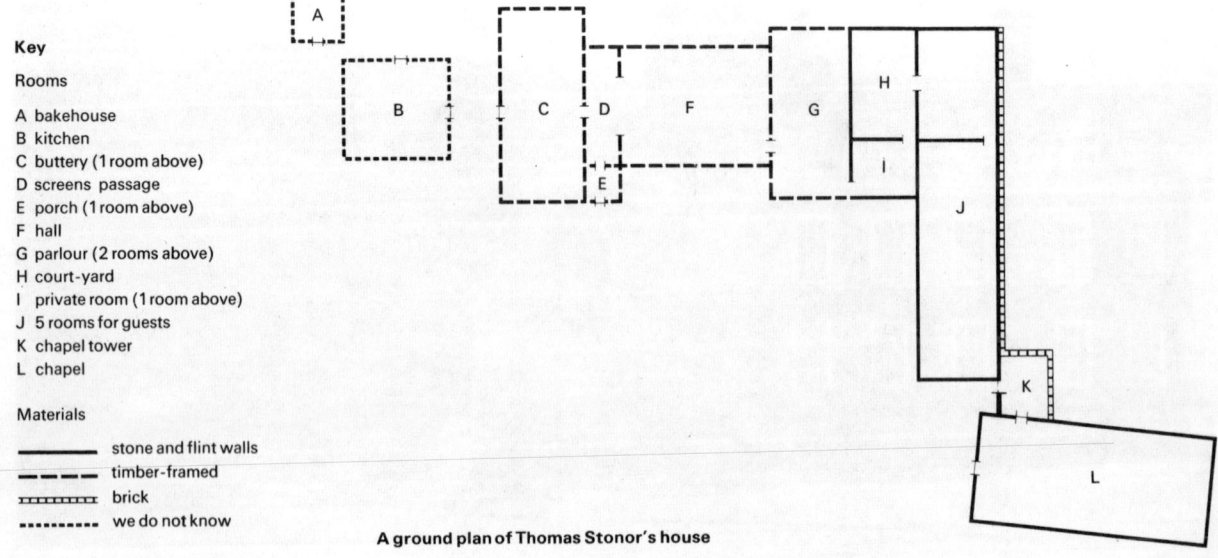

Key

Rooms

A bakehouse
B kitchen
C buttery (1 room above)
D screens passage
E porch (1 room above)
F hall
G parlour (2 rooms above)
H court-yard
I private room (1 room above)
J 5 rooms for guests
K chapel tower
L chapel

Materials

———————— stone and flint walls
– – – – – – timber-framed
xxxxxxxxx brick
············· we do not know

A ground plan of Thomas Stonor's house

How Stonor Park grew

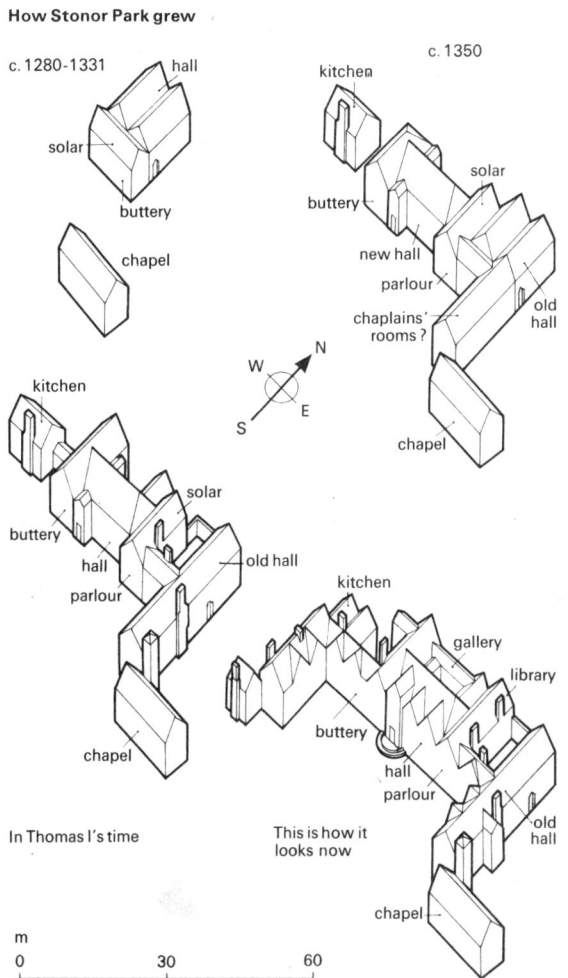

c. 1280-1331
- hall
- solar
- buttery
- chapel

c. 1350
- kitchen
- solar
- buttery
- new hall
- parlour
- chaplains' rooms?
- old hall
- chapel

W N E S

In Thomas I's time
- kitchen
- solar
- buttery
- hall
- parlour
- old hall
- chapel

This is how it looks now
- kitchen
- gallery
- library
- buttery
- hall
- parlour
- old hall
- chapel

m
0   30   60

It was a group of eight or nine buildings, not just one.

Nowadays if we want more room we usually have to move house, but men like Thomas Stonor stayed put. There was plenty of land so all they had to do was to add a few buildings.

Use the diagrams to make your own models of Stonor Park. You could use a collection of boxes and label them to show how the house grew.

A fifteenth-century hall

11

Building in brick

What is your house made of? I expect it is made of bricks because today most people live in brick houses. But in Thomas's time, nobody in Oxfordshire had a brick house. All were made of wood or stone. The name Stonor means 'a stony ridge', and the first parts of the house were made of stone, timber and flints from nearby. But Thomas knew that there were many brick houses in Flanders, and also quite a few in England itself – in East Anglia. We don't know how far he had travelled, but he may have seen them for himself. So he decided he would build the very first brick house in Oxfordshire. In the year 1416–1417 he bought 200 000 bricks from a man called Michael Warwick at Crocker End, near Nettlebed. You can find these places on the map in this book. There is still a brick kiln at Nettlebed. Two things made this a good place for making bricks—clay and fire-wood. Perhaps you can find out how bricks are made. Here are fifteenth-century brickmakers at work.

What colour are the bricks used in your neighbourhood? If you go to another part of the country you may notice the bricks are a different colour to those at home. Why?

Thomas got men from Flanders to make and lay the bricks. What country is Flanders in now? Here are builders at work (below and right).

As later members of the Stonor family added bits to the house after Thomas, we are not sure of all that Thomas had built in brick, but we do know two things. He had a tower built to join the private chapel to the house. This had bricks arranged in a trellis pattern, using burnt bricks as the darker ones. And a wall in the house was built with bricks specially moulded in the shape of hearts and flowers.

Alms

While he was building the house and chapel, Thomas did not forget his neighbours who were worse off than he was. He had an alms-house built in Assendon. How far was this from his own house? (Find it on the map.) This was to provide homes, board, lodging and pocket-money for nine blind and feeble men. Assendon was, and is, a small village, so this alms-house must have taken people from all over Oxfordshire and other counties too. You could look at a map and see where the people might have come from. Giving alms was partly to help others, and partly because Thomas Stonor wanted to do something which he thought God would like him to do.

What does the word 'alms' mean? The alms-house at Assendon is no longer there, but there are many others. Have you got one near you? Do old people live in it? How old is it? Who gave the money to build it? (You will often find this information on a wall plaque.) Who pays for the rates and repairs? Are there other special places where old people live? Do you think it is a good idea to have alms-houses for the blind or old?

Do a survey to see how many buildings near you have bricks arranged in patterns. Draw the patterns; some older houses have fancy yellow or grey bricks arranged with red ones. Most brick walls are arranged in simple patterns. Discuss with your teacher the difference between English bond and Flemish (from Flanders) bond as shown here.

English bond

Flemish bond

A wedding and a lot of lands

The other good thing about having your own chapel was that you could have weddings there. And that brings us back to the wedding of Thomas Stonor.

Thomas married Alice Kirby. She came from a place called Horton Kirby, near Dartford in Kent. Her father was a rich man and Alice was his only child. When her father died, Alice was heir to his lands at Horton. This was a good farm of 2000 acres, reaching as far as the river Thames. Thomas already had many farms and lands far bigger than Horton in the south of England. They were in nine different counties and some were a long way from Stonor Park.

It was usual to have lands scattered about the country. If one farm was attacked by cattle rustlers or had a bad harvest, Thomas would still have food or money from other places. Also, once a man had land, he was not always buying and selling: the eldest son inherited the lands when his father died and generation after generation owned the same land and lived in the same house, just like Thomas Stonor. His wealth was in land.

> How many times bigger than your school playground is 2000 acres?

Here is a list of his estates:

Berkshire	Beansheaves in Tilehurst (near Reading), Buscot, Didcot, Earley, Englefield, Sotwell
Buckinghamshire	Land at Bierton (near Aylesbury), Stoke Mandeville, Walcote, and a little farm near Fawley called Mousehols
City of London	A house in the lane of St Peter the Little, near Paul's Wharf
Devonshire	Ermington
Gloucestershire	Bourton-on-the-Hill, Condicote, Doughton, Harnhull, Henbury
Hampshire	Foxcott, Penton Mewsey
Kent	Horton Kirby
Lincolnshire	Repinghale, Walcot
Oxfordshire	Bix, Pishill, Pyrton, Rycote, Stonor, Thame, Watcombe, Watlington
Westminster	A house called 'The Moot' with 60 acres, a barn, 3 cottages, and a shop

> Look at the list of the estates. Use a gazetteer and a map and find out where all these places were. Mark them on a map of your own. Measure the distance between them. If you were Thomas Stonor going on a tour of your lands, which would be the longest part of the journey? Could you do it on horseback in a day? How many places were near a river or the sea? Why did this matter?

Thomas travels

A man owning all those lands had to keep an eye on them, so Thomas had to travel a good deal. The year after he married Alice, he went off to look at his new estate at Horton Kirby.

The journey from Stonor to Westminster was an easy day's ride and they could stop at 'The Moot'.

> Look up 'The Moot' in the list above. How far was it from Stonor?

Crossing London

As Thomas had to go south of the River Thames to reach Horton Kirby, he had to make for a bridge and this meant going through the City of London and across London Bridge. At first his way lay through pleasant country lanes. He passed a plot of land called Scotland, a church called St Martin-in-the-Fields and the village of Charing. Then to the fashionable area of the Strand where there were houses with gardens running down to the river. When he got to Temple Bar he knew he was nearly in London. The City had walls all round it, but houses and shops had been built outside the walls, and the City people had put posts and chains across the roads leading into it to mark the boundary line. These were called 'Bars'. Thomas crossed a dirty river called the Fleet and entered the City through Ludgate. The view he saw is above right.

The City was packed with people, horses, and carts; the houses and shops were close together; the drains smelled and there was a terrible din. When Thomas reached London Bridge, it was jammed with traffic. (Can you think why?) As it was lined with shops and houses, he could only occasionally catch a glimpse of the River Thames between them.

Once across the river, Horton Kirby was only a short ride from London.

Trace Thomas Stonor's journey on your map.

Make a model of old London Bridge. It had nineteen arches. Round cheese boxes cut in half would make good arches. Then you could put the houses and shops on top. Look carefully at the pictures to get the right style of building.

London celebrates a victory

On the way home Thomas got caught up in a frenzy of excitement. The King, Henry V, had just won a great victory against the French at the Battle of Agincourt, and all London turned out to welcome him home. This is what an eye witness said:

'When the Saturday dawned the citizens went out to meet the king at the brow of Blackheath, i.e. the mayor and twenty-four aldermen in scarlet and the rest of the citizens with red and white party coloured hoods to the number of 20 000 horsemen. And about ten o'clock the citizens rode towards the City and the king followed.'

The bridge and other key points in the City were gaily decorated with banners and emblems. A chorus of young girls dressed in white came out to greet the king singing, 'Welcome Henry the fifth, King of England and France'. The trumpets and horns sounded. There was such a dense throng of people in Cheapside that horsemen had scarcely room to ride through the crowds, and the upper storey windows were filled with people.

Agincourt was one of the most famous battles in the long wars the English fought against France and which we call The Hundred Years' War. Perhaps all this excitement made Thomas wish he could go and fight too. He did go abroad a few years later, but we don't know whether he fought in a battle.

> Make a picture or collage of the scene in London. Act the scene.
>
> Find out more about The Hundred Years' War and especially the Battle of Agincourt.

Henry V

a man he particularly trusted, called the Chancellor. He only called Parliament when he wanted to discuss such things as going to war, making a new law, or asking them for a tax. He had to have a fair sized hall to fit them all in. He used a hall in the Palace of Westminster, or one in St Peter's Monastery.

You can see a Parliament sitting here. The king sits on the throne and the lords and bishops sit near him on the left of the picture. Some are sitting on four woolsacks in the middle. Try to

find out why they are woolsacks and you will be able to say 'I know' later in the book. The men in front of the picture are the 'commons'. The man standing in the centre is their Speaker, a very important man. When Thomas Stonor was a member of parliament, the Speaker was his guardian, Thomas Chaucer.

This picture was drawn in 1523 but Parliament looked much the same in Thomas Stonor's time.

Thomas Stonor first went to Parliament when he was only twenty-two, as member of parliament for Oxfordshire. He went six times altogether, but not always to Westminster.

Westminster

Although he did not like London much, Thomas did like Westminster. Westminster is now a part of inner London, but in his day it was a country place. The king had a palace there which was conveniently near to the most important city in the land, but much nicer to live in. The palace, like Thomas Stonor's house, was not one building, but several. Some were used by the king to live in, and for entertaining foreign princes and the great men of his own kingdom. Others were used as government offices and law courts. Close beside the palace was the great monastery of St Peter, with grounds running down to the River Thames. What part of the monastery is still there?

Parliament

In those days Parliament was not held at regular times, nor even always in the same place, but wherever the king happened to be.

When the king wanted to talk over important matters with his subjects he sent for them. He summoned the lords (princes, dukes, earls, bishops, lords) and the commons (two knights from each county and two citizens from each big town). He had no cabinet or prime minister because in those days it really was the king who ruled, although he was usually helped by

> Parliament means 'having a talk'. What other words beginning with 'parl' do you know? Look in a dictionary.

17

Lord of many manors

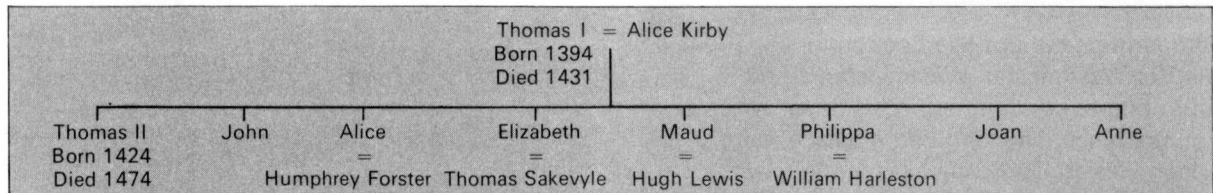

			Thomas I = Alice Kirby Born 1394 Died 1431				
Thomas II Born 1424 Died 1474	John	Alice = Humphrey Forster	Elizabeth = Thomas Sakevyle	Maud = Hugh Lewis	Philippa = William Harleston	Joan	Anne

Orphans

As Thomas Stonor's son had the same name as his father, it is easy to get confused. So we shall call them Thomas I (the first) and Thomas II (the second). This is the way we distinguish between kings and queens with the same name.

When Thomas I died in 1431 his children were orphans. There were a lot of orphans in the Middle Ages. Looking back through this book can you find two reasons for this? Yes, you are probably thinking of illness as one reason. Both grown-ups and children, rich and poor, often died of diseases which would not kill us. For instance, without antibiotics like penicillin, they could die of pneumonia, and without antiseptics or knowledge of surgery, they could die of appendicitis. They had other 'killer' diseases – smallpox, and the Black Death or pestilence. Even rich people lived in much dirtier conditions than we do. They lived much rougher lives, but they took it all for granted.

Praying for deliverance from the plague

You may even think some things in their lives were better than ours when you have read all through this book.

When Thomas I was ill and knew he might die, he arranged for his guardian, Thomas Chaucer, to be a guardian to his own children. The girls were to be married if possible, and if not, to enter convents. It was usual for a father to arrange his children's marriages. You can see from the family tree which ones got married.

Thomas I arranged for his sons to be educated; Thomas II would inherit all his father's lands, and John was to have a house and land at Buscot (Berkshire). Before Thomas II was nine, Thomas Chaucer died, for he was an old man. By that time Alice Stonor had married a second husband, Richard Drayton, and they all lived together at Stonor..Alice and Richard had more children so there was quite a big family.

Ewelme

The Stonor family kept up the friendship with the family at Ewelme. Thomas Chaucer's daughter, Alice, lived there with her husband, William de la Pole, Duke of Suffolk. So the Stonors had a Duke and Duchess, very wealthy and grand people, for their friends. While Thomas II was still in his teens the Suffolks started a great building programme at Ewelme. They built a manor house for themselves, a church, a school and an alms-house. There was no social security or state education, so those who could afford it, gave their money to help others. All these buildings, except the house, are still there, and still used for their original purpose.

If you live near Ewelme, try to go and see it. If not, read the story about a boy who lived there. It is by Cynthia Harnett and is called *The Writing on the Hearth*.

Son-in-law to a duke

When Thomas II grew up he married one of the Duke of Suffolk's children, Jane. Thomas II and Jane had three sons and three daughters. The eldest son was called William.

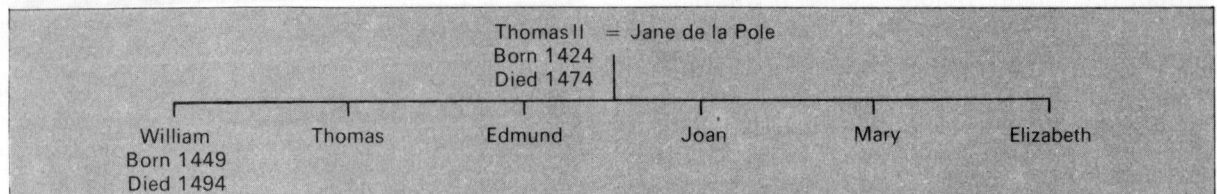

Thomas II = Jane de la Pole
Born 1424
Died 1474

William	Thomas	Edmund	Joan	Mary	Elizabeth
Born 1449					
Died 1494					

Look carefully at the names in this and the earlier family trees. Who are the children named after? Whom is William named after?

How did your parents decide what name to give you? Make a chart showing the most popular Christian names in your class. Or, better still, do a survey of the whole school. Which are the 'top ten'? Then do a survey to find the most popular names among your parents. Has the fashion in names changed? Why?

And what about surnames? Who has the name of a place (like the Stonors), or of an occupation (like Brewer or Carpenter)? Make a list. Can you get more than six surnames like this in your class? How many more can you think of? In what other ways did surnames start?

A murder

The year after William was born there was a murder in the family.

William's grandfather, William de la Pole, Duke of Suffolk, was a tough old soldier and the most important adviser of the King, Henry VI. But his efforts to make peace with France made him unpopular and he was even accused of trying to murder Henry's brother. After a great fuss in Parliament, the King banished him from England for five years. The Duke tried to cross to France in his ship, but just as he was leaving Dover, a gang of fishermen kidnapped him, put him in a rowing-boat and cut off his head.

You can imagine the shock and horror Jane and Thomas felt when they heard this news.

This picture of the Duke's murder was drawn in 1802

Wars of the Roses

Plots, murders, sudden fights between neighbours, and even battles, were common at this time. The trouble was that Henry VI was not a strong ruler and everyone was trying to influence him to suit themselves, especially the princes. One branch of the royal family, descended from King Edward III's son, the Duke of Lancaster, had been kings of England since 1399. Now, their right to the throne was challenged by a branch descended from another son, the Duke of York. The Yorkists had a white rose as their badge and the Lancastrians later took a red rose as theirs. So this feud was known afterwards as the Wars of the Roses.

In spite of this unrest, Thomas and Jane Stonor lived quietly and peacefully during the Wars of the Roses, as did many other people. When William grew up things were different, but that comes later.

Scores of sheep

You will remember that the wealth of the Stonor family was in its lands. Therefore they depended on either growing crops, or keeping animals to sell at a profit, or on letting land for rent. Thomas Stonor had great flocks of sheep — hundreds of them — on the Chiltern Hills near Stonor, in Hampshire, and in the Cotswolds near Bourton-on-the-Hill. Several crops were grown on the estates, but the sheep were more important — not for their meat, but for their wool.

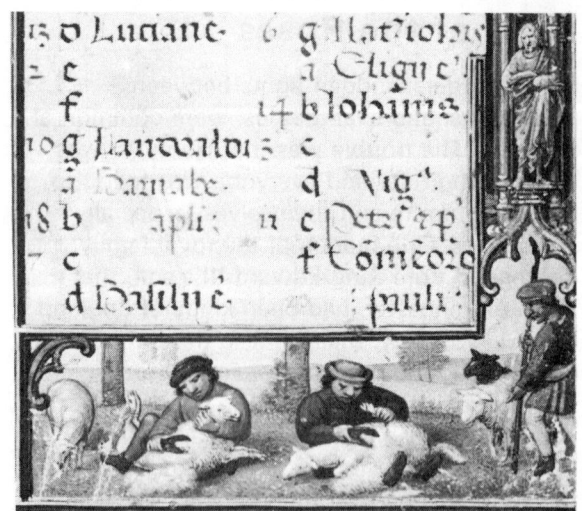

The farm at Horton, which Alice Stonor had inherited, had fewer sheep than at Bourton or Stonor. However, the sheep had to be sheared here too. It cost 22d. to shear 12 score and 9 sheep and 6d. to shear 8 score lambs at Horton.

This way of reckoning the numbers of sheep and this kind of money are not used now, but there are still older people who remember what 'a score' means. How many sheep and lambs were there at Horton?

Counting sheep

The shepherd could not read or do sums on paper, but he had a special way of counting his sheep. He made them pass between hurdles in pairs. As they passed he recited his special counting words like this:

onerum
  twoerum
    cockerum
      shuerum
        sligerum
          slatherum
            wineberry
              wagtail
                tarrydiddle
                  den

As he did so he cut a notch for each on a tally stick like this:

What other counting rhymes or words do you know? Make a list. If you want more, look in the books by I. and P. Opie and Walter de la Mare, listed at the end of this book.

If he was counting in pairs, how many sheep did he have, and what is the old word for it? Cut yourself a tally stick and try it out with people going through a door. Ask your teacher to help you find out what else tally sticks were used for.

How many other meanings does the word 'score' have?

It was not only the big landowners who kept sheep. Some quite poor men had a few sheep and on 27 December 1460 Thomas Stonor arranged to lease some sheep to a man called Simon Cook. Simon Cook was to have 4 score ewe sheep (worth 12d. each) for four years, for which he had to pay Thomas Stonor 26s. 8d. in two instalments. Simon Cook could breed from these ewes and keep the lambs, so it was cheaper for him than buying his own.

If you now know all about scores and old money like 's.' and 'd.', you will be able to work out how much it would have cost Simon Cook to buy the ewes.

Wool

Wool was then the main, or staple, product of England: some was woven into cloth in England, but much of the raw wool was sold to foreign merchants. In the House of Lords in London there is a large object in front of the throne. It is the Woolsack, and on it sits the Lord Chancellor of England when Parliament is in session. This shows how important wool was to England for many hundreds of years. When Thomas Stonor stayed in London in 1463 he slept at an inn called The Woolsack in Fleet Street.

Some towns have inns or hotels called The Fleece or The Lamb, or streets called Sheep Street, and our language is full of words and phrases connected with wool and cloth. A phrase for telling a story is 'spinning a yarn'. Can you make a list of such words, phrases and names? When you have finished see if you can beat the list on page 47.

Cloth

Although the Stonors sold nearly all their wool, they had some woven into cloth on their own estates. When Jane Stonor wanted hard-wearing cloth woven, she sent wool from the Stonor sheep to the weaver at Watlington, near Stonor. His name was William Demnyst. He sent it all back woven and dyed. In 1468 he charged 2d. to make 16 yards of white broadcloth, and 1d. for making 12 ells of russet kersey.

Broadcloth was fine but tough, and kersey was rough. Find out what an ell was. What colour was russet? Where else do you find this word?

Thomas Stonor's servants had a lot of clothes made of russet kersey but they also had black and yellow ones, and some in Kendal-green, a special green cloth made at Kendal in the Lake District. These clothes had to be made at home, and the Stonors paid extra people to come in and have great sewing sessions to help do all the work. The finest clothes for Thomas and Jane, and best clothes for the children were made from material imported from the continent. English weavers made mainly the hard-wearing everyday cloth.

What colour cloth were Robin Hood's men dressed in? Kendal-green is an example of giving the name of a place to something which makes it easy to recognise. Other examples are Lancashire hotpot and Cornish pasty. How many more can you think of?

You could try spinning. Gather some sheep's wool from the hedges and try twisting and pulling it to make a long thread. If you want to weave, it will be easier with bought wool. Why not make a piece of russet-coloured cloth? You could investigate the spinning and weaving of cloth thoroughly and make an exhibition to show the different processes. You could also experiment with making your own dyes by boiling leaves and berries. Then dye a piece of white material and label it in your exhibition showing which leaf or berries you used.

Trouble at Ermington

With so many estates, some producing food, some wool, and some being let for a money rent, Thomas Stonor needed to employ quite a number of men as managers. Each estate had a bailiff — the manager on the spot.

But, like his father, Thomas II still rode about on horseback visiting his various estates and the bailiff kept a bedroom ready for him. There were some things which only he could decide.

of to the Stonors. Poor John Frende, who was supposed to collect the rents, got the worst of it. He wrote to say:

'Fortescue and his men are threatening me so that I fear to go out to church or shopping, or even about the farm. I'm afraid to leave the house. You promised to come down and see about it and I really can't stand any more. If you don't come at once I shall resign.'

The tenant comes to pay his rent

When Thomas's eldest son, William, was thirteen, Thomas had an urgent letter from John Frende, the bailiff of Ermington in Devon. There was trouble with the Fortescue family again! The Fortescues were a rich family of landowners in Devonshire who had been quarrelling with the Stonors on and off for years, about who owned Ermington. Now, Richard Fortescue was trying to make the Ermington tenants pay their rents to him instead

He did not resign, though, and one day Fortescue and his men kidnapped John and locked him up for four days until he paid a ransom to get out. John Frende and Thomas Stonor took Richard Fortescue to court over this and the court said Richard was in the wrong. But this trouble kept boiling up like a pan of potatoes, and it was only settled years later when Thomas's granddaughter married a Fortescue.

26

It was difficult to keep law and order at the best of times. There was no national police force and local people had to be responsible for catching criminals. There were proper courts in each county and the king's judges came round periodically, just as they do now. But, as you know, the country was not well governed at this time. Some of the wealthy people (like the Fortescues) kept small private armies on their pay-roll, who wore a special livery or uniform to show whose men they were. They looked rather like Securicor men.

Sometimes, like the Fortescues' men, they took the law into their own hands. If you have ever seen a 'Western' where men did this in a lonely district, you can imagine what it was like. Ermington was a lonely district, just south of Dartmoor. And of course it was so far from Stonor that it was not easy for Thomas Stonor to keep his eye on it all the time.

In your school are there children who take the law into their own hands? Are there gangs like the men who wore the Fortescues' livery? If you were in a school which was not well governed, how would you improve things? Pretend you are John Frende and write a letter to Thomas Stonor telling him about the kidnapping. Are you going to resign this time?

Dogett

The journey to Ermington would have taken Thomas Stonor several days. If it had been necessary for him to visit all his estates often, he would never have been at home. However he had a top manager, who supervised the bailiffs, called the Receiver. The man who had this job when William Stonor was born was named Henry Dogett, and he kept the job for nearly forty years. He was an educated man, responsible for collecting the rents, doing the accounts, arranging repairs, arranging to sell the wool from the sheep and many other things besides. He had a clerk called Gerveys and a servant to carry messages, so he was not what we would call a servant. But when he wrote to Thomas Stonor he signed himself, 'Your old servant, Harry Dogett'. This was a form of politeness. When Thomas wrote to him he addressed him as, 'My old friend'. Harry Dogett had to travel a lot of course, but he bought himself a farm at Pusey in the Vale of the White Horse (Oxfordshire) and kept sheep and sold the wool like his master. On the wall of Pusey church you can still see a plaque in memory of Henry (who died in 1491) and his wife.

Pretend you are Harry Dogett and write a letter to Thomas Stonor telling him all you have been doing during the last month. You can describe your route to Ermington and back. You could stop at a Stonor house each night if you find all the estates on a map.

The outdoor life

Thomas II and his family rode everywhere.
The horses went to be shod by a smith at
Assendon, and the same smith shod the oxen
that were used to pull the carts and ploughs.
These were used more than horses for farm
work. Oxen were used for ploughing until
quite recently.

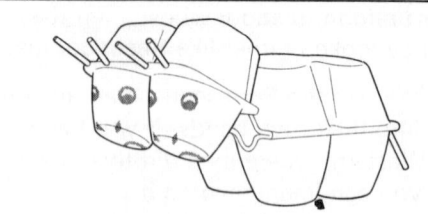

You could make a pair of oxen from an
egg box. Use pieces of felt, wool, card
or paper for the horns and tails.
Oxen are still used in some parts of the
world. Can you find out where?

The Stonors, like all medieval men, liked hunting. They hunted animals they could eat — deer,
hare and wild boar. The word 'park' originally
meant a piece of land which was fenced to
keep in the deer. So the name Stonor Park
shows it was used for hunting. There are deer
in the park still, and a strong fence. The Stonors
kept packs of greyhounds to chase the deer
and used crossbows to shoot them. Of course,
the deermeat or venison was food for the
family, and sometimes they sent venison as a
present to their friends in London. But it was
sport too, and sometimes for a change they got
permission to hunt somewhere else. The King
had huge areas reserved for hunting.
Although these areas were called forests, they
were not rows of trees, but tracts of rough
grazing land with plenty of bushes and small
trees to provide cover for the animals. The royal
foresters looked after the King's forests and
poaching was severely punished.

Can you make a list of forests still left in
England? What are they used for now?
What sort of forest does the Forestry
Commission plant, and what is it used for?

28

The Stonors used mastiffs to hunt wild boars and then rushed in and finished off the boar with a special branched boar spear. Another sport was hawking. They trained falcons to fly at herons, mallards and partridges.

Sometimes they got permission from the King to go hawking at Woodstock where he had a palace, a park and a forest. There were different kinds of falcons: the peregrine, the merlin and the hobby.

Thomas II and his sons also liked the sport of baiting animals. There was bull-baiting, bear-baiting, and even horse-baiting; and they liked cock-fighting too. They played football, with no rules and a game called 'curling'. Do you know where this is played now?

You may have read the book *A Kestrel for a Knave*, or seen the film *Kes*, about a boy who trained a kestrel hawk.

While the falcons were moulting, or mewing, they were kept in buildings called mews. Later the king's mews were turned into stables for horses, and the name mews came to mean stables at the back of a big house. Find out where there are mews buildings. Usually they will be in a town. What are they used for now? Do you know any other buildings which are used for something for which they were not originally built?

The stay-at-home

Thomas II's wife, Jane, went out with the family when it was not too far. To get to Reading they had to cross Caversham Bridge. There was a sacred well at Caversham, where they could drink the water, and a shrine on the bridge. Nearby was one of the greatest monasteries in the land, Reading Abbey with its shrine to St James. Ask your teacher why people visited shrines. Parliament was sometimes held here. (In what other abbey was Parliament held?) The Stonors could buy wine at Reading Fair and go on to visit one of their estates (which one?).

But Jane liked home best. Once when Thomas II had been on a round trip to Devon and then stayed in London, he wrote to her saying he wanted to bring a visitor home to stay. She wrote, 'Better shut up house than take visitors. Servants are not so diligent as they used to be.' And she told Thomas to hurry up and come home, because it was not good for the children never to see their father. She added a P.S. 'please remember the gentian, rhubarb, silk, caps, pots, leather laces, an ounce of embroidery silk, laces and treacle.' She addressed it to him at The Sword in Fleet Street.

The spring in Caversham was a chalybeate spring. What is this? Why do people go to a spa? Make a list of six spa towns in Britain.

Why did Jane send the shopping list to Thomas instead of going herself?

The funeral

Thomas II was fifty years old when he died. Look up the date. He had lived longer than his father or his grandfather, and because he was so well known he had a grand funeral. He was buried at Pyrton Church. How far from Stonor was this?

A feast was given for the guests and here is part of the shopping list and menu:

For poor men: umbels to make broth, roasted well in a dish together with roast beef and roast pork.

First course for priests etc. broth, capons, mutton, geese, custard.

Spices: 1lb saunders, 1oz saffron, 3lbs pepper, ½lb cloves, a loaf of sugar, ½lb ginger, 3lbs currants, 3lbs dates.

Wooden vessels for poor men, pewter vessels for gentlemen, spoons of silver for the most worshipful men.

Remember milk, chickens and eggs.

What is gentian?
What do you learn from this list about:
a) the kind of food?
b) the amounts. How much pepper does your mother buy?
Do you think they had the feast at home? What did the poor men go without at the feast? What were umbels? Sometimes they were made into a pie. What does the saying mean 'eating humble pie'? How do you think the two are connected? What other words in this book have changed their meaning?

Three years before Thomas Stonor died his contemporary King Henry VI died. There was no funeral feast for him. He was murdered in the Tower of London. Edward IV was already King before Henry died and he ruled well until 1483. Both kings are buried at Windsor Castle in St George's Chapel.

The merchant of the staple

When William Stonor inherited his father's estates, he was only twenty-four years old. Nevertheless, he had plenty of opportunity to learn how to run the estates before he had to take over. He used to go out with his father and listen to him carrying out his business. Thomas II was a very strict man with his tenants and his children.

There were other changes too. William's mother, Jane, went off to live at the family estate at Penton Mewsey in Hampshire, and eventually died at Henley, where she is buried in the churchyard. His two brothers, Thomas and Edmund, went off to fight in France for a little while. From France they wrote William letters, and Edmund used a monogram for his surname, as you can see in the picture. Edmund Stonor did his monogram in two ways.

You could try to make a monogram for yourself with the letters of your own name, or initials.

Elizabeth

William quickly found himself a wife. In the summer of 1475 he married a London lady, Elizabeth Ryche. She was rich too. She was not an aristocrat, but she was generous, loving, and full of fun, and William must have been glad he married her. She had servants to do the housework, but she had to organise them and manage the housekeeping, and she was rather scatter-brained about all that.

A house full of children

Elizabeth made Stonor Park a merry, noisy place because she loved having visitors to stay and she filled the house with children. She was a young widow when she married William Stonor and had four young children. Here is another instalment of the family tree. But remember these are *Ryche* children, not Stonors.

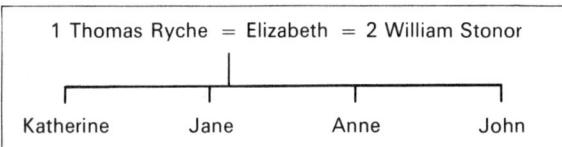

1 Thomas Ryche = Elizabeth = 2 William Stonor

Katherine — Jane — Anne — John

In 1477 Elizabeth became the guardian of four more children (two boys and two girls) whose father, an old friend of hers, had died. These were Fenn children. Then William became guardian to several more orphan children. William and Elizabeth Stonor had no children of their own, but even so there were altogether about eleven children in the house, as well as all the boys working in the stable and about the farm.

Shoeing the family

William bought shoes as well as clothes for his workers and servants. Between them all they wore out a lot of shoes. All the shoes were made to measure by hand, and the shoemaker sent in a bill for the year 1478–1479 for 75 pairs of shoes for the children. At the same time William ordered himself a long pair of boots to the knee and a pair of galoshes for Elizabeth. The shoemaker never ran short of leather because he was able to use the skins of the many animals which were kept at Stonor.

Elizabeth's galoshes were made of wood and metal, rather like platform-soled shoes, to wear over her other shoes to keep her feet out of the mud.

Some people nowadays have galoshes or Wellington boots, made of rubber or plastic, but there was no rubber or plastic in the Stonors' time. Can you make a list of things which we have, made of plastic or rubber and then find out what they would have been made of if the Stonors had had them? You could make a list in columns like this:

Now	My grandmother's time	The Stonors' time
plastic washing-up bowl	enamel	wood

Eating and drinking

Elizabeth fed her family well. It 'snowed meat and drink' in her house. Most of the food came from their own farms or gardens. They could have plenty of pork, poultry, honey, apples, pears and homemade bread. There was no refrigeration or tinned food and not much food for the cattle to eat in the winter. So they had to slaughter many animals in the autumn, have a great feast, and put the rest of the meat into great tubs of salt brine. They could have salmon in season from their own fishery on the River Erme, if anyone was coming up from Devon. At home they had fish ponds rather like the fish farms which are now being tried out again. They kept pigeons in dovecotes for eating and their own chickens for eggs. And of course there was some food got by hunting and hawking.

When Elizabeth wanted extras she bought them from the cottage people near Stonor or in Watlington. When candles were needed, a man from Watlington came to Stonor for several days, to make hundreds of them out of mutton fat, which Elizabeth supplied. This arrangement was rather like the one Jane Stonor had over the weaving of cloth. The best candles, for the solar and the chapel, were ordered from a London candle-maker who used wax.

Imagine you are living in an isolated farm, cut off from the rest of the world by floods. How will you survive when the stores run out? What food will you eat and how will you get it? What will you use to make clothes when yours wear out? How will you keep warm? What will you do in the evening when it gets dark? (The floods have cut off the electricity supply.) You can read how other people managed in this sort of fix in *Robinson Crusoe* by Daniel Defoe, in *The Swiss Family Robinson* by J. Wyss or in *Castaway Christmas* by M. J. Baker.

But they had to buy some things from other parts of England or from abroad. They paid porters to carry what they bought to the wharf at Queenhithe on the River Thames and load it on to a barge. The bargemaster was William Somers and the Stonors paid him to bring their goods to Henley. Why do you think they sent things by water and not by road? On 9 May 1476 a barge left London at noon and got to Henley four or five days later. When the things got to Henley they were unloaded on to pack-horses to be taken to Stonor Park.

Here are some of the things bought in this way:

6 bundles of rushes
A gown of silk from Padua
Two brass bowls
3 barrels of herrings (each containing 600)
50 salt dried cod
A sackful of fruit
8 bunches of garlic
2½lbs sugar
3 pecks of green peas
1 butt of Romney wine, price £4
1 rondelet of Malmsey
200 oysters

Where did some of the things like fish, wines, ginger and sugar come from?

Make a model of a barge. Load it with the goods and put William Somers the bargemaster on it.

Many goods were bought at fairs.

Make a frieze for the wall showing all the people and goods at a fair. There is a very good description of a fair in Rhoda Power's story *Redcaps Runs Away.* Ask your teacher to read it to you.

Make a list of ten fairs still held in your area, using M. Baker's book *Discovering English Fairs.* What happens at a fair now?

The words it 'snowed meat and drink' are in quotation marks because they were written by Geoffrey Chaucer who wrote *The Canterbury Tales.*

Off to court

Elizabeth stayed in London a good deal. This was natural as her relations and many of her friends lived there. She had grown up as a Londoner: her father, her first husband and many of her family were rich merchants and among the top men in the City of London. Some were mayors or aldermen. So Elizabeth was used to a gay city life with plenty of money, friends and travel. But however rich and important merchants and their families were in London, they were not regarded as quite so 'high class' as the country gentry. William Stonor had something which Elizabeth wanted very much — friends and relations connected with the great lords and invitations to the King's court. The most important of these people was John, Duke of Suffolk. The family tree shows you the connections.

Elizabeth once went to a house party at Windsor Castle. There was hunting in the forest, a tournament in the park and dancing in the evening. No wonder she was extravagant over clothes. One dress length was 38 yards of green sarsenet at 5s. a yard (compare this with Thomas's bill on page 7). The London merchant from whom she ordered it wrote, 'Madam the sarsenet is very fine. I think it most profitable and most worshipful for you, and shall last you your life and your child's after you.' He was probably right. Materials in the Stonors' time were of very good quality and people did pass them on to their children or give them away.

> Look back through the book for all the information about clothes. Dress up as characters in this book. You can make your clothes or borrow them from the County Drama Wardrobe. If you can't dress up, make a collage for the wall.

This is how Elizabeth looked when she attended the Duchess of Suffolk.

William de la Pole, Duke of Suffolk = Alice Chaucer

John, Duke of Suffolk = Elizabeth, the sister of King Edward IV   Jane = Thomas II

William = Elizabeth Ryche

Writing home

When Elizabeth was away from home she wrote William a lot of letters. Here is part of a letter Elizabeth wrote:

Right entirely and best beloved husband, I recommend me heartily unto you. And now for your good venison and conies, which you sent me by Harry Blakhall, which is great dainties to have here in London; wherefor I sent the half hawnch to my father and a couple of conies. I have been with my Lady of Suffolk and went with her to see the King and Queen. And good sir, I pray you that my blue gown of damask may be sent to me in time for Hallowe'en with my other gear. I have not heard from my son Betson for no boat has come in for eight days. Your children and mine fare well, blessed be God. No more at this time, Almighty Jesu preserve you in long health and virtue.

At London the xxii October.

My own cousin I send you a Bladder with powder to drink when you go to bed, for it is good for you.

By your own
Elizabeth Stonor

To my Right well-beloved cousin William Stonor, Esquire, at Stonor, this be delivered.

When is Hallowe'en? Why doesn't she give a date? What is a coney? What is gear? Why did Harry Blakhall take the venison?

This is the way Elizabeth actually wrote the last three sentences:

My owne cosyne, I sende you a bladyr with powdyr to drinke when ye go to bed, for it is holsome for you.

By your owne
Elysabeth Stonore

To my Ryght well-belovyd Cosyn Wyllm. Stonore, squyer, at Stonore, this be delyveryd.

You will have noticed that Elizabeth in her letter calls William 'cousin'. This was a term of affection which just showed you knew someone well.

Look at the lines in the spelling Elizabeth actually used. Try reading them aloud and you may be talking rather like the Stonors did. They did not have a fixed way of spelling, but wrote as it sounded to them. How are the beginning and end of Elizabeth's letter different from the way we write letters?

Now you have seen several extracts from the Stonor letters. Be Elizabeth and write to William, describing your visit to Windsor. You could use a monogram or a signature. Instead of using an envelope, fold the letter and seal it with sealing-wax, just as Elizabeth did.

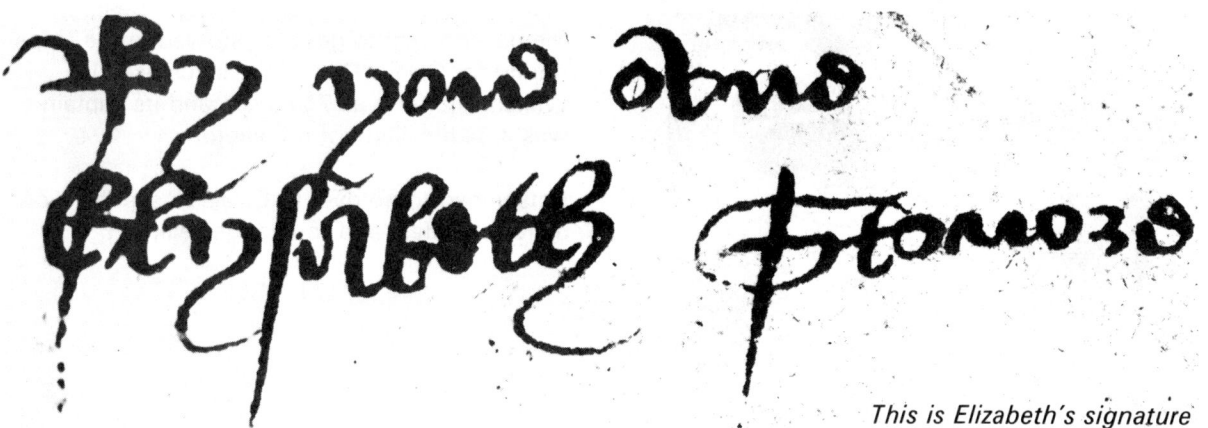

This is Elizabeth's signature

The merchant of the Staple

Marrying Elizabeth changed William's life. As you know his family had always been large-scale graziers, selling the wool and other products from their farms. But they had always been country gentlemen. Now William became a merchant as well. Instead of selling his wool to dealers to export to the markets of Europe, as his father had done, he got pack-horses and ships, and began to buy wool from other graziers and send it abroad himself. He went into partnership with Thomas Betson and became a merchant of the Staple.

The Staple

The Staple was a special market, where English wool for the rest of Europe had to be sent. This was in one fixed place, at Calais, which belonged to England. Only merchants who were members of the Company of the Staple could sell wool to foreigners, and this could only be done at Calais. So William Stonor was joining a select trading club. It was a good arrangement for the merchants because they could keep the business to themselves, and they could also join in sending convoys of ships to protect each other against the pirates who swarmed the English Channel.

The wool-packers

William employed several people to ride round the country buying up wool. Thomas Betson also did a lot of this. He often went to big wool markets at Northleach in the Cotswolds, and rode all round the farms in Gloucestershire, Hampshire and Oxfordshire to buy wool direct from the graziers. He then paid a deposit and arranged for it to be packed and sent off. There were rules made by the government and the Company of the Staple to make sure there was no cheating. Once sacks of wool were found to be padded out with thistles! The wool had to be packed by a man from the Fellowship of Wool-packers from London. It was then stamped with a special mark and carried by a train of pack-horses along the old trackways over the chalk hills of southern England to London. There it was taken to the Leadenhall, where it was weighed at the King's Beam. Next the packers had to get it all stowed in the ships bound for Calais. One of the ships used by William Stonor was *The Jesu*, and its captain was a man called John Lollinton.

Betson had to go over to Calais to see the wool delivered safely and to arrange selling it.

Merchants' marks

Every bale had a merchant's mark stamped on it. This is the one William Stonor and Thomas Betson used.

Can you read the words which come before the merchant's mark?

Where else in the book can you see this merchant's mark?

To my ryght
worshypffull and syngular
good mayster
William Stonore Esquyer
Soyt d.d.

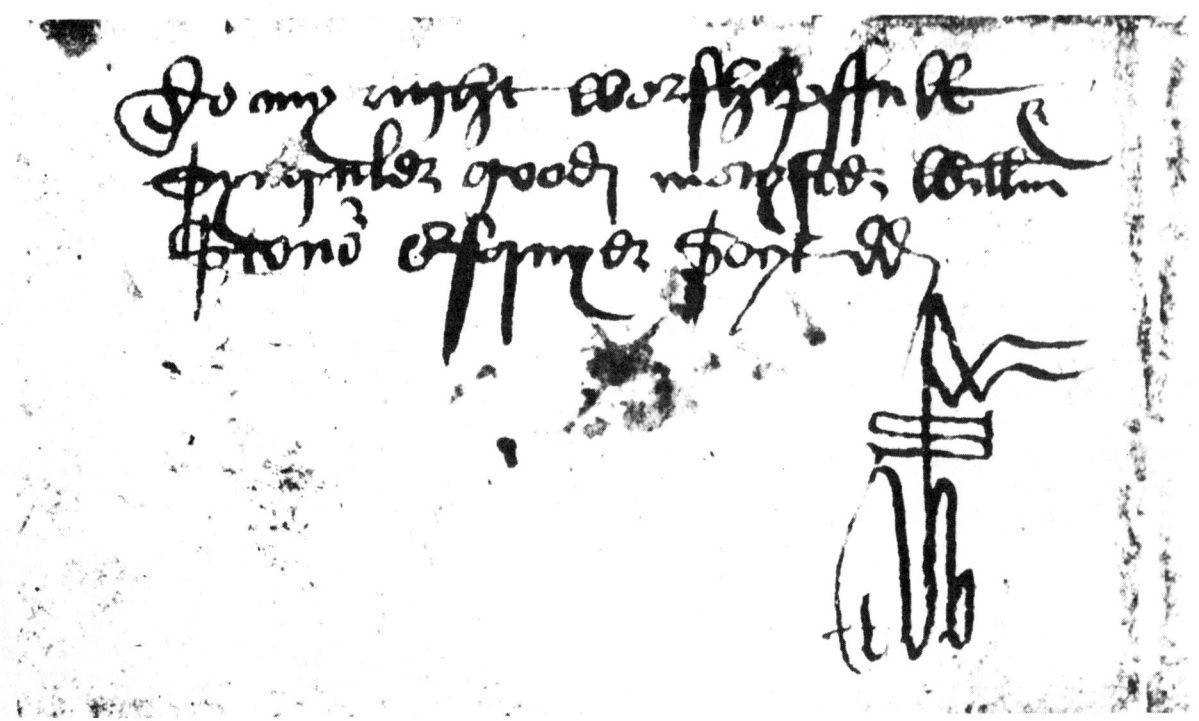

This was to make the bales easy to identify. The dockers could not read but they could recognise different marks. Also, most ships carried the goods of several different merchants, and if they were sunk, the marks would make it easier to sort out the contents if they were washed up on a beach.

Merchants also used their marks in the same way as the gentry used their coats of arms, because they were proud of being merchants. They put their marks in glass windows, on seals, on tombs and brasses.

Can you find Leadenhall Street on a map? The name is connected with the King's Beam and both are connected with weighing. Can you find out what sort of scale this would be? How does it work? Could you make a model of it to show how scales work? Make your own merchant's mark.

Arranging a marriage

Thomas Betson was not just a business partner to William Stonor: he was a family friend and he married Elizabeth's daughter, Katherine. So he really was her son, as it says in the letter on page 37. When Katherine was only thirteen years old she was engaged to Thomas. As you know, parents arranged marriages for their children, and perhaps the two people did not always get on. Thomas Betson really did love Katherine very much, but he was a grown man and he had to wait for her to grow older to marry him. This is part of a letter that he wrote her from Calais, wishing she could be grown up sooner. He began,

> 'My own heartily beloved cousin Katherine' and went on, 'If you would be a good eater of your meat always, so that you might grow fast to be a woman you would make me the gladdest man of all the world, by my troth. I pray you greet well my horse and pray him to give you four of his years to help you and when I come home I will give him four of my years and four horse loaves to make amends.'

And he sent her a ring.

They were married when Katherine was nearly sixteen and went to live in London. Here is a picture of them in the garden.

If you find the joke about the horse's years confusing, you could discuss it with your teacher. If you were Katherine, would you like that way of writing, or would you rather he had just said, 'I wish you were older'?

As Thomas Betson was a London merchant all his life, he and Katherine were buried in the Church of All Hallows, Barking-by-the-Tower. If you go to the church now you can see brasses in memory of several wool merchants, because this was in the merchants' part of London, but not those of Katherine and Thomas.

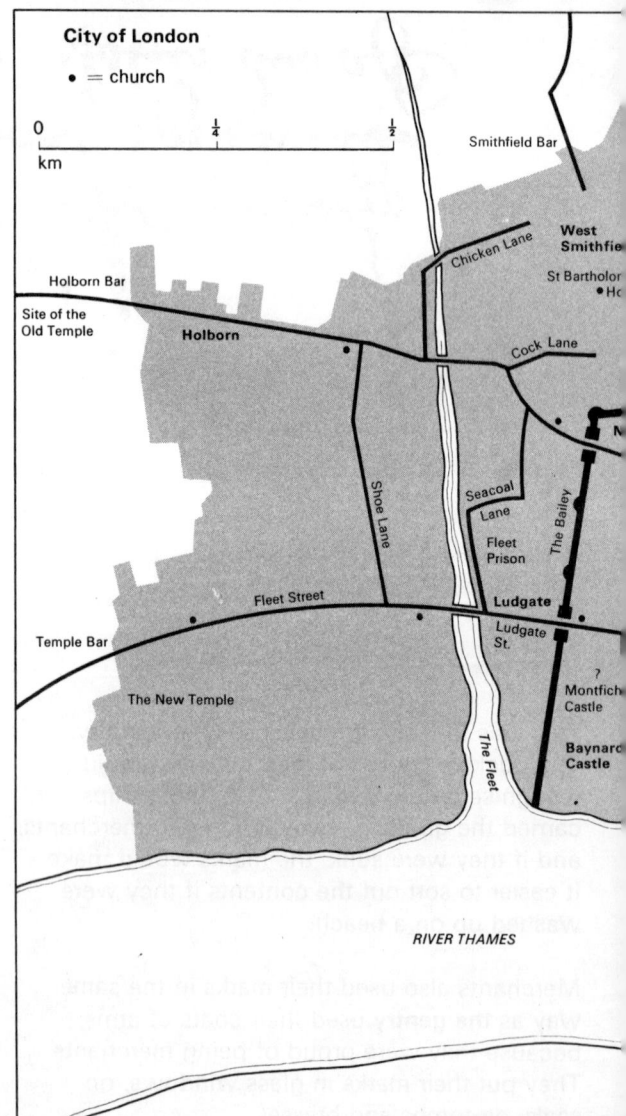

City of London

• = church

0   ¼   ½
km

Smithfield Bar

Chicken Lane

West Smithfie[ld]

St Bartholo[mew]
• Ho[...]

Holborn Bar

Site of the Old Temple

Holborn

Cock Lane

Shoe Lane

Seacoal Lane

The Bailey

Fleet Prison

N[...]

Fleet Street

Ludgate

Temple Bar

Ludgate St.

?
Montfiche[t] Castle

The New Temple

Baynard Castle

The Fleet

RIVER THAMES

The City

This section is a do-it-yourself one.

By now you have had several pieces of information about the City of London. (Look back carefully at the whole section on William and pages 15–17.)

Compare the map with a modern one. How many streets have the same names?

How many 'bars' and 'gates' were there around London? Make a list.

'Cheap' or 'chipping' indicates a place where things were sold. How many 'cheaps' in London? Are there any streets in your town called 'Cheap' or 'Market'? Can you list twelve towns containing the word 'chip', 'cheap', 'chepe' or 'chipping' in their names?

Now, imagine you are William (who, as a merchant, spent more time in the City than his father and grandfather), and write a letter to a friend in the country describing a typical day of your stay there.

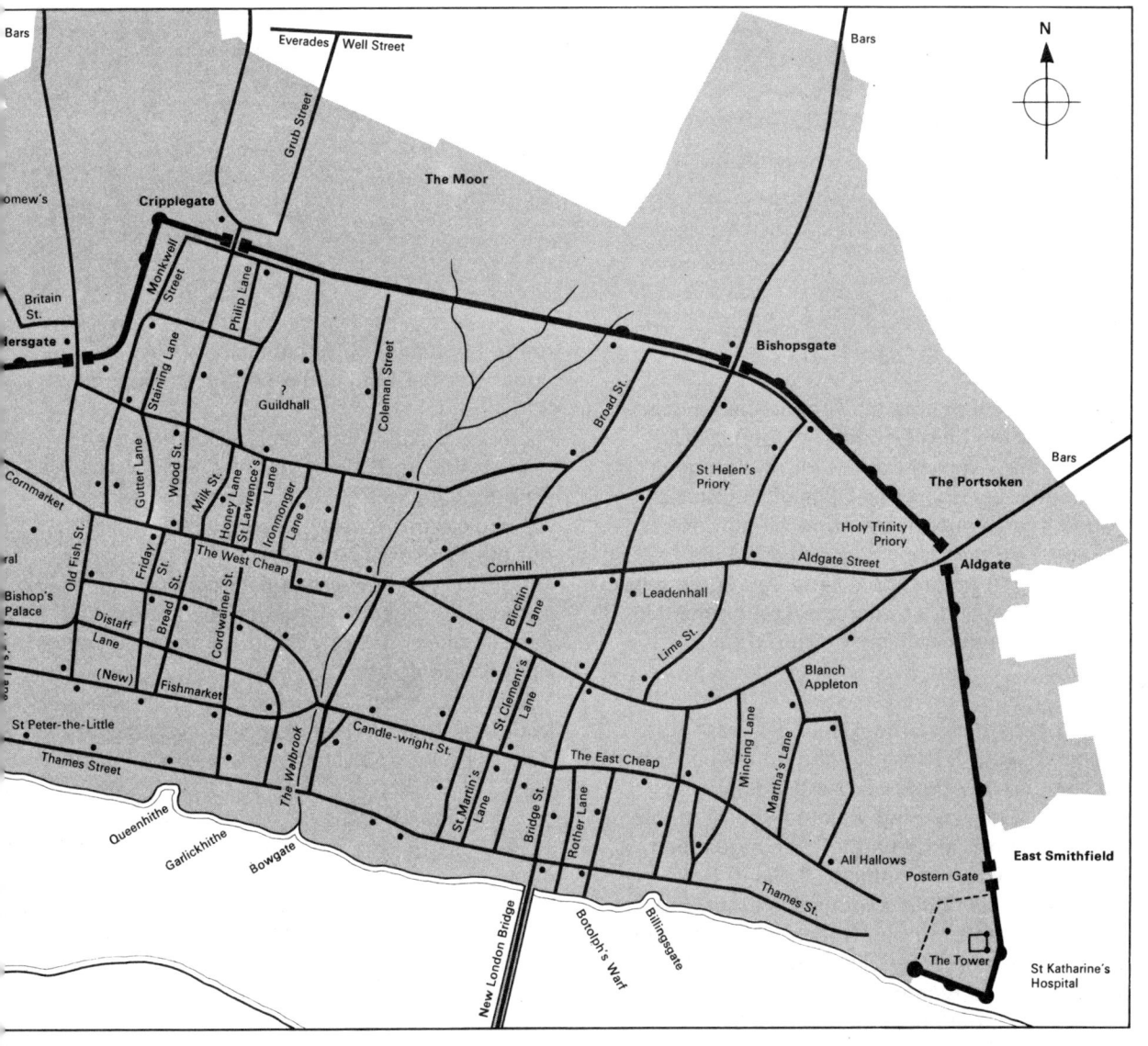

The worshipfullest of all the Stonors

William sold his Westminster house, but he still attended the King's Parliaments, just as his father and grandfather had done, and he was at the King's court more than either of them. He was a very ambitious man. The powerful Duke of Suffolk (John) and his wife (Elizabeth) helped him to go to court and meet the King.

In 1478 William was made a Knight of the Bath and soon after he was a Knight of the King's Body. This meant he was often with the King to talk to him, amuse him, and take important messages. William was such a successful man that a friend called him 'The worshipfullest of all the Stonors'. Here is William's signature. Notice the 'K' after his name which shows he was a knight.

The King's guardian

This was the first time the Stonors had much to do with the King's court and soon William found himself mixed up in a lot of plotting. You may remember about the Wars of the Roses. You will remember about strong King Edward IV. You will remember William de la Pole executed in a rowing boat. And you know what quiet lives William's father and grandfather led. Well, this is how William got mixed up in politics.

The crisis came in 1483. (How old was William?) King Edward IV died on 9 April, when his son and heir Prince Edward was twelve years old. The boy King was too young to rule England alone, so he had to have a guardian. This guardian was his uncle, Richard, Duke of Gloucester, his father's younger brother. But Prince Edward's mother, Queen Elizabeth, and her relatives, the Woodville family, hoped that, although Duke Richard was the guardian, they themselves would have the biggest say in

ruling England. For, of course, whoever controlled the King could control the kingdom.

As far as Duke Richard was concerned there was no time to be lost. The twelve-year-old King Edward was staying at Ludlow Castle with his uncle, Lord Rivers (a Woodville), when he got the news that he was the new King. So he set off for Westminster to get ready for his coronation. Duke Richard met the young King and his uncle at Stony Stratford; he imprisoned Lord Rivers and the boy was taken to the Tower of London. The Tower was then a royal house and not just a prison, so there was no need for anyone to start worrying yet.

Trace on a map the journey of young King Edward from Ludlow to the Tower. How long would it take travelling 40 miles a day?

Meanwhile the young King's mother, and his younger brother Prince Richard, were staying at the Royal Palace at Westminster. When they heard what had happened they went to the Sanctuary of Westminster Abbey and stayed there. The Queen was frightened and the Sanctuary was a place where she could ask the Church to protect them.

To the Tower

And well she might be frightened. June was a month of terror. Richard, Duke of Gloucester, pretended that the young King Edward was to be crowned and he made the Queen hand over her younger boy, Prince Richard, to join Edward in the Tower to await the coronation. Meanwhile he had several of the Queen's family executed or imprisoned. He spread the rumour that the Queen was not properly married to the old King, Edward IV, and so her son was not the true King of England. On 6 July there was a coronation. But, it was not the young prince who was crowned, but Richard Duke of Gloucester, who was crowned King Richard III of England.

What of the Princes in the Tower? In October they were seen shooting and playing in the garden of the Tower, but day by day they were seen more rarely behind the bars and windows; and soon the two little Princes in the Tower were dead. It seems likely that they were murdered, but who did it? If you go to the Tower of London now, you will see the White Tower. Here, in 1933, doctors examined the skeletons of two boys: they said one was aged twelve or thirteen, the other about ten—just the ages of the Princes in the Tower.

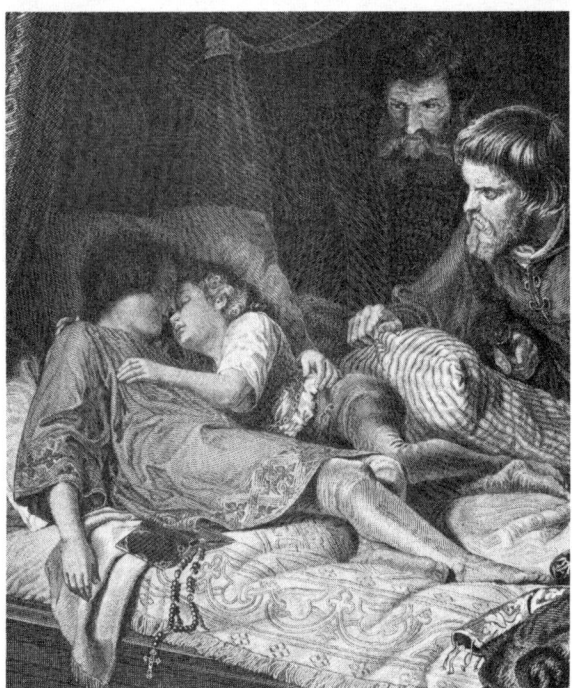

Rebellion

Now where did William Stonor come in? Well he was a tolerant man and he saw Richard III crowned without complaining. But by October, round about the time the Princes disappeared, he joined with some important men, led by the Duke of Buckingham, in deciding that this King Richard would have to go. They organised a rebellion: groups of armed men from different counties planned to take over at Westminster and choose a new King, Henry Tudor. William Stonor and Sir John Norris led the rebels in Berkshire.

But the whole rebellion failed and the King had the Duke of Buckingham executed, for rebellion was treason. (Ask your teacher about this.) William Stonor fled abroad, probably to Brittany. King Richard couldn't get hold of William, but he took away all his lands and let other people have them. We do not know what William's family did in this terrible time, but they probably went with him. But not for long.

On 1 August 1485, Henry Tudor, Duke of Richmond, came from France, with an army. He had many supporters, including William Stonor. There was a battle on 22 August at Bosworth Field.

At Bosworth King Richard was killed and Henry Tudor was proclaimed King of England.

Aerial view of Bosworth Field. The circle marks the centre of the battle area.

Can you agree between you what parts you'll play, and turn this story into a play and act it? You could also make a model of the Tower of London showing how difficult it was to escape from. And if you like war games with model soldiers you could stage the Battle of Bosworth.

You can find Bosworth Field if you follow the signpost just outside the town of Market Bosworth in Leicestershire. What is the field used for now?

Henry Tudor could claim to be King because he was descended from Edward III, but really, he became King because he won the battle; and he stayed King because he ruled England well. And that was the end of the Wars of the Roses. The King married Princess Elizabeth (of the family of York) and so the two families who had been at loggerheads for so long, were united.

Look up the Royal Family tree in a history book to find out exactly why Henry Tudor could claim to be a descendant of Edward III. Was Elizabeth of York also descended from him?

William comes home

William Stonor got all his lands back and went home to Stonor. And he too settled an old quarrel. Do you remember the trouble at Ermington? William married his daughter to Adrian Fortescue and his son to Mary Fortescue. So there was no more quarrelling down in Devon.

The historian at work

Later members of the Stonor family had very exciting adventures, but there is no room for more in this book. Although the Stonors lived so long ago we know a good deal about them. But we do not know everything. In order to find out about people in the past we have to be detectives, following up clues and asking questions. We look at a house and wonder who lived there. We read the letters the family wrote. We cannot see the same shoe that William Stonor paid for, but we can find one like it in a museum. We cannot see Westminster as Thomas I saw it, but we can look at a map and try to imagine it. We can go to Stonor Park and see the very view the Stonors saw. You can do this sort of thing near home. Start with a building or a tombstone or a few letters. Then keep asking questions and following up clues. If you do this you will be historians yourselves.

Things to do

In the past people made rubbings of brasses in churches. Now the brasses are getting badly worn and so the best place to go if you want to rub a brass is a brass-rubbing centre like the ones at Oxford, Gloucester and London. Practise first on coins, textured wallpaper or, if you can find them on a pavement, coal-hole covers.

Here is a picture of Ewelme Church, which you will remember was built by William de la Pole. How many different things can you see in it? What are their names? How many of them can you find in your parish church? Try and find out why the church was divided into two parts.

46

Badges

Here is a list of people or organisations with coats of arms or similar badges. Can you add to it? The Queen, families, colleges, universities, county councils, regiments, the Royal Navy, the R.A.F., inns and hotels, trade unions (banners).

Sheep

Here are a few words and phrases used in everyday speech, and some surnames and place names connected with sheep, wool and cloth.

Words and phrases
pulling the wool over his eyes, spinster, tease, to fleece, wool-gathering, sheepish, like a lot of sheep, making sheep's eyes, fleecy clouds, dyed in the wool, to unravel a mystery, cloth ears, clothes, fuller's earth, shepherd's pie, sheepshank, the black sheep.

Place names
Ewelme (Oxfordshire)
Kersey (Suffolk)
Sheepy Parva (Leicestershire)

Surnames

Fuller	Sheppard
Shearer	Weaver
Shepherd	

Some books for you to read:

Crush, M. *Costume* (First Look at Series, Franklin Watts 1972)
Donoughue, C. *The Development of Writing* (Jackdaw 1967)
Harnett, C. *The Wool-pack* (Puffin)
The Writing on the Hearth (Puffin)
Hindley, G. *Medieval Warfare* (Wayland 1971)
Hunt, P. J. *What to Look for Inside a Church* (Ladybird 1972)
What to Look for Outside a Church (Ladybird 1972)
Hunter, E. *The Story of Furniture* (Ladybird 1971)
I-Spy Churches (Dickens Press 1966)

Lewenhawk, S. (ed.) *The History of Wool in Britain* (Jackdaw Publications 1972)
Loxton, H. (ed.) *The Battle of Agincourt* (Jackdaw 1966)
Westminster Abbey (Jackdaw 1967)
Mare, Walter de la (ed.) *Come Hither* a collection of rhymes and poems for the young of all ages (Puffin 1973)
Power, R. *Redcap Runs Away* (Jonathan Cape 1971)
Tales from Chaucer retold by Eleanor Farjeon (Oxford University Press)
Taylor, B. (ed.) *Saxons, Middle Ages and Tudors* (Brockhampton Press 1973)
Trease, G. *Bows Against the Barons* (Brockhampton Press 1966)
Bent Is the Bow (Salamander Books, Nelson 1965)

Those marked * are stories

Books for the teacher:

Baker, M. *Discovering English Fairs* (Shire Publications 1968)
Bennett, H. S. *The Pastons and their England* (Cambridge University Press 1932)
Cunnington, C. W. and P. *Handbook of English Medieval Costume* (Faber 1952)
Ekwall, E. *Concise Oxford Dictionary of English Place Names* (Oxford University Press 1960)
Holmes, G. *Later Middle Ages* (Nelson 1962)
Iredale, D. *This Old House* (Discovering Books, Shire Publications 1968)
Janitch, V. *Fun with Historical Doll Making* (Kaye and Ward 1973)
Kingsford, C. L. (ed.) *The Stonor Letters and Papers 1290–1483* (Camden Society Third Series vols. XXIX & XXX)
The Observer's Book of Heraldry (Warne 1966)
Opie, I. and P. *The Lore and Language of Schoolchildren* (Oxford University Press 1959)
Reaney, P. H. *A Dictionary of British Surnames* (Routledge & Kegan Paul 1958)
The Origin of English Surnames (Routledge & Kegan Paul 1967)
Withycombe, E. G. *The Oxford Book of English Christian Names* (Oxford University Press 1973)

Table of dates

1327–1377	**Edward III**

1354	*Sir John, the judge, dies*
1368	*Sir Ralph is born*

1377–1399	**Richard II**

about 1387	Geoffrey Chaucer writes 'The Canterbury Tales'
1393	*Gilbert is born*
1394	*Thomas I is born*
	Sir Ralph dies
1396	*Gilbert dies*

1399–1413	**Henry IV**

1404	This book begins

1413–1422	**Henry V**

1415	*Thomas I marries Alice Kirby*
	Battle of Agincourt

1422–1461	**Henry VI**

1424	*Thomas II is born*
1431	*Thomas I dies*
1434	Thomas Chaucer dies
1448	*Thomas II marries Jane de la Pole*
1449	*William is born*
1450	William de la Pole, Duke of Suffolk is murdered

1461–1483	**Edward IV**

1474	*Thomas II dies*
1475	*William marries Elizabeth Ryche*
	Alice de la Pole, Duchess of Suffolk dies
	William Caxton prints 'The Canterbury Tales'

1483	**Edward V**

1483–1485	**Richard III**

1483	*William rebels and goes abroad*

1485–1509	**Henry VII**

1485	Battle of Bosworth Field
	William comes home

Entries in italics refer to the Stonors